POEMS FROM HOME:
A CHILDREN'S ANTHOLOGY

There will be times when you walk into a room and no-one there is quite like you...until the day you begin to share your stories. And all at once, in the room where no-one else is quite like you, the world opens itself up a little wider to make some space for you.

-Jacqueline Woodson, The Day You Begin

To the children...

Each and every one of your poems has made me smile; you should be so proud of the poetry you have created. The amount of talent and imagination in these pages is wonderful and I'm so happy that your work is being shared with other people. I've read about your pets, your likes and dislikes, your favourite days, your favourite people, the depths of your imaginations, and a fair bit of poo! You have mastered acrostics, haiku, limericks, free verse and more. You are all incredible. Thank you for sharing your work, and for trusting me with it.

To the adults...

Thank you to the adults who have encouraged your children to take part and submitted their work. This has been a group effort and your involvement has been hugely appreciated. This is our first edition and hopefully the first of many.

To Matthew Buckley...

Thank you for your hours of work editing pictures and creating the front cover for our first edition. Same time next year!

Jennifer Buckley, Editor

LIST OF AUTHORS

Holly A   1
Juwairiyah Ahmed   2
Ramin Ahmed   3
Nour Ahmida   4
Sara Ahmida   5
Peter Andrews   6
Alethea Archer   7
Emel Askar   9
Imaan Askar   10
Kawther Askar   11
Isabelle B   13
Jack Shelton Baker   14
Jack Baker   16
Louis R Baker   17
Theo Barback   18
Eden Barnes   19
Niamh Barnes   22
Harvey Bartlett-Rawlings   23
Harry Charlie Bench   24
Jacob Blockley-Walker   25
Nicole Bourne   26
Elias Jun Choi Bowers   27
Luca and Maximo Bradbury-Ross   28
Samuel Bradley   30
Harrison Brewer   31
William Brodzinski   32
Aidan Brown   33
Elijah Buckley   35
Calliope Buckley   36

Charlotte Chillman	37
Jesse Chillman	38
Dylan Cole-Reeve	39
Rose Cole-Reeve	40
Chloe Cuzick	41
Isobella Davis-Healey	42
Poppy Davis-Healey	43
Marco and Logan Drew	44
Jess Duggan	45
Lilly Elwardany	47
Eva Firnigl	49
Luke Freemantle	50
Mya Freemantle	51
Stanley Galloway	52
Grace Gannon	53
Raven Rain Gaskin	54
Hayley Gerber	55
Robyn Gerber	56
Caleb Oliver Grant	57
Iris Grant	58
Alex H	59
Olivia H	60
Millie-Ray Halpin	61
Owl Halpin	62
Evelyn Hardy	63
Keira Hardy	64
Eve Harris	65
Indie Hartland	66
Asiyah Alice Hassane	67
Jessica Anne Hatt	69
Aazer Hirst-Khadir	70
Musa Hirst-Khadir	72

Salar Hirst-Khadir	73
Shuky Hirst-Khadir	74
Yuunis Hirst-Khadir	78
Tiffany Horton	79
Toby Horton	81
George Hurd	82
Harmonie-Rose Husk	83
Melodie-Eve Husk	85
Arthur Hutchinson	88
Dottie Hutchinson	89
Tilly Hutchinson	90
Saaliha Jackson	91
Zahra Jackson	92
Anna Johnson	93
Alina Jones	94
Leya-Rose Jones	95
Summer Jones	96
Phoebe Kelly-Jack	100
Raphael Kneller	101
Stella Koenig	102
Augustine Kwon	104
Sophia Lane	105
Sebastian Le Mesurier	106
Thomas Le Mesurier	107
Alia Longhurst-Hills	109
Siri Longhurst-Hills	110
Arlo Blue Maguire	111
Eadie Bea Maguire	112
Oryn Hazel Maguire	114
Hifzah Mahmood	115
Rafaella Markham	116
Ruben Markham	117

Ahlehgra-Neroli Mattherson 118

Santino Mattherson 119

Tiano Mattherson 120

William McCauley-Tinniswood 121

Jasmine Mclauchlan 123

Ruby Mclauchlan 125

Xander Middlemiss 126

Zoë Middlemiss 127

Maddison Milne-Emslie 128

Ruben Milne-Emslie 129

Lucy-Kate Myers-Lowe 131

Johan Oosthuizen 132

Darwin Overton 137

Seren Overton 138

Nivedita Pattni 139

Niyati Pattni 140

Aibhlinn May Pearson 141

Ciara Jane Pearson 142

JJ Petch 143

Beatrix Pilmer 144

Cordelia Pilmer 145

Phoebe Piloni 146

Penhaligon Price-Davies 147

Ettienne R 148

Yasmin Reeves 149

Emma "My Little Pony 150

Sophie" My Little Pony Lover", 152

Aletheia Xinyue Ruan 153

Persephone Xinxiao Ruan 154

Sophie S 155

William Simmonds 156

Taffie Smith 159

Joseph Stanton 161

Hanna Thanweer 162

Elana Tufft 164

Harrison Tufft 165

Maya Tufft 166

Evangeline van Vuuren 167

Eliza Varley 168

Ava Waddingham 169

Bobby Wells 171

Evelyn West 173

Finn West 174

Bonnie Wilgrove Hewitt 175

Olly Wilkinson 176

Boo Williamson 177

Jackie Williamson 178

Katelyn Williamson 179

Luna Wilson 180

Oscar Woolford 181

Eva Woolven 182

Clara-Elizabeth Worton 184

Finlay Worton 185

Joshua 187

Zachary 188

Jet 189

:SWINGING IN THE TREE:

I love swinging in the tree,
I can see everything!
I can see the tree,
I can see the branches,
I can see the leaves,
I can see the sky,
I can see the sunshine,
I can see the clouds,
I can see my friends,
I can see my teacher,
I can see my mummy,
I can see the brambles,
I can see the grass,
I can see the fire circle,
Swinging in the tree.

- Holly A, 6, King's Lynn

:UNICORN WORDS:

Stand by Unicorns
But he bumbles
and fumbles
and tumbles,
Door, floor bumbles.

- Juwairiyah Ahmed, 5, Birmingham

:ALLEY FOOTBALL:

The game starts
And Muhammed grabs the ball
And calls
To Matt who shows off his smarts.

But what's this!
He gets tackled by Jack
Who jumps over the cat ,
And flicks over Matt
And Nate saves his

shot. Oh no! It's gone over to Nat's
We knock and Nat says "Hello?"
" Can we get the ball? " we say
"OK but do u know what name I should give to the cat?"

A few minutes later it's 4:4
And there's 1 minute until we go
So Mohammad flicks , tricks and megs the defender
Nothing can stop him and with his right foot he curves the ball into
the goal!!
GOOOOOOOOOAL!!!

Ramin Ahmed, 10, Birmingham

:KINDNESS:

Help people
Give toys to kids
Speak good
Play with children
Be nice to orphans
Be respectful
Be kind to elders
Give your parents flowers
Share your things
Make people happy
Have good manners
Give food to people

- Nour Ahmida, 7, Middlesbrough (from Libya)

:CARING:

Take care of animals
Take care of nature
Eat healthy
Recycle to help animals
Give birds food & water
Be nice to your mummy and daddy
Play games with your mummy and daddy

- Sara Ahmida, 5, Middlesbrough (from Libya)

:THE WITCHY DITCHY:

Bubbles up from top to bottom
It soils from every ground
Snow falls everywhere
Add an egg and lots of hair
Put your books - stir, stir, stir
Just a spoon of feathers
Sticks, sticks, sticks
Swirl and swirl, add a bone
Put a bone, add some spiders
From top to bottom
Add some nails, it has to be painted
Add some sugar, nice and fainted
Add some flour, it has to be sweet
Loads of whiskers and one eye
You need loads of spots from a tiger,
Stripes from a zebra,
Sticks from a frog
Some lily pads and mermaid scales
Put a hat and snow and cherry
Bury, bury, bury them, bury, bury, bury
From all that stuff, it's the end!

- Alethea Archer, 6, Leigh-On-Sea

:ICE CREAM:

YUM! YUM! YUM!
Ice cream in my tum!
Yummy yum yum!
Ice cream YUM!

- Emel Askar, 5, London

:THE LONELY STONE:

I am a stone
A hard, hard stone
I'm all alone
And I am unknown.

- Imaan Askar, 8, London

:HAPPY OR SAD?:

I'm happy
and don't try to convince me that
I'm miserable
because I can tell you that
I'm as jolly as can be
so don't say
I'm sad
for I really am not
say I'm happy

(Now read the lines in reverse)

- Kawther Askar,10, London

:BOOK:

Your nose stuck in a book.
Just take a look!
It will take you to a brook
Where you will meet a crook
Sitting in a nook
Reading his book
To learn how to cook.
Just take a look!
You'll see a man fishing with his hook
By the brook.
He fished up a rook
Got scared and shook.
When you have your nose stuck in a book.

- Kawther Askar,10, London

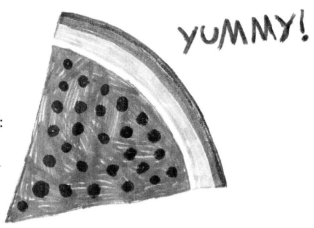

YUMMY!

:WATERMELON:

Watery wonder
Amazing
Terrific
Excellent, extraordinary, exquisite.
Red, round and refreshing
Munch, munch, munchy melon.
Eating it is exciting
Large, lovely and lime-green
Oval orb
Nice to nibble

- Isabelle B, 8, Aberdeenshire

:AS I SIT HERE:

As I sit here in the **Heather** patch,
Looking up towards the sky,
a **Heron** passes me by.
The **Willow** tree blows the **Dandelion** fluff
that scatters like dust all over the **Bramble** bush.
The **Conker** tree stands so tall,
I wonder how many will fall.
The **Fern** rustles, the **Ivy** creeps
as the **Weasel** tries to sleep.
The river flows without dismay.
Otters play in the month of May.
Newts hide from the **Kingfisher's** eye.
The **Larks** sing, what a beautiful thing.
The **Wren** bobs about doing its own thing.
The **Raven** sits and watches quietly.
The **Starling** looks for food with all its might
as the **Magpie** sees something bright.
Bluebells dance in the spring sun,
Looking as if they are having so much fun.
An **Acorn** drops with a flop.
The **Adder** slithers here and there without a care.
All this as I sit here and stare,
wondering why no one cares
that these words are almost not there.
Please take care and please be aware,
I fear these words may never reappear.
Look for these words as they might hide
but if we remember them, surely they'll never slide.

- Jack Shelton Baker, 14, Sheffield (Written aged 11)

:THE DOG RESCUE:

I was sat waiting to be rescued
I hear footsteps, I wag my tail,
Maybe it's my turn to be adopted.
Woof Woof Woof, I shout as the
footsteps get closer, Woof Woof,
The footsteps have gone past. I wag my tail,
Woof Woof they've stopped but it's not for me.
I don't woof, I don't wag my tail.
I just lay down listening, because
Maybe, just maybe, next time,
the footsteps will adopt me.

:MY MOM:

My mom is my mom and I love my mom
My mom is lovely
My mom is squishy.
I love my mom and my mom loves me
My mom gives me hugs
and gets rid of all the bugs
My mom wipes my tears
and dissolves all my fears.
My mom is my mom
and I love my mom and
My mom loves me.

- Jack Shelton Baker, 14, Sheffield

:O X E Y E D A I S Y:

Oxeye daisies are very white, they are also very bright,

Xmas tree? It is not, lavender? It is not, it is the one, the only, oxeye daisy with its bright yellow spot!

End of an oxeye daisy, it may be sad, but cheer up, as another seed might land,

You will often see them so make sure you always greet them,

Envelope? to send us to a friend, or even keep oxeye daisies until the end,

Do some yoga with us oxeye daisies, if you are really that crazy, but remember to leave us a glass of water or two as we would really like that from you,

Apple tree? It is not, clover? It is not, it is the one, the only, oxeye daisy with its bright yellow spot!

Ill knee? I see, well I have the perfect thing from me, oxeye daisy bump balm, just remember, DON'T EAT!

Smell me, sell me, or even take pictures of me, there are lots of things to do with oxeye daisies,

You must never forget me, for I am the one, the only oxeye daisy!

- Jack Baker, 11, Spalding

:SHENFIELD IN THE RAIN:

There was a train,
In the pouring rain,
The train goes clitter, clatter, clack,
The rain goes pitter-patter back,

Puffing goes the train through that wet weather,
And the rain just kept getting heavier,
The train's windows were soaking,
Some of the passengers were moaning,

But just then...

The sun appeared from behind the clouds,
Quietening the rain so loud,
Until it was no more,
And the train with its carriages, four,

Trundled into another sunny field,
Where the birds sang so loud,
And the train made its stopping sound,
As it pulled into a station

- Louis R Baker, 9, Beckenham

17

:PEGI RATINGS:

Pegi ratings on the Switch
Pegi 18s will make you twitch
Pegi 18s aren't suitable for kids to be having
Cause of the horror, zombies and all of that stabbing

Pegi 16 are big men fighting in a ring
Knocking your tooth out, making ears ping
When you hear gunshot you can see blood
And some soldier down on the mud

On Pegi 12 there is online chat
So, strangers calling you "a big fat bat".
Proper monsters you've got to slay.
Those monsters aren't making your day.

Pegi 7s are for kids, but they're harder maybe
Compared to 3s they're a little more scary
Little kids might find them tough
7s are just a little bit rough.

Pegi 3 is the minimum age
Just painting walls the colour beige
There's no peril and nothing grating
Let's just say it's the baby rating.

Pegi ratings will keep you safe.
Trust Pegi ratings, you've got to have faith.

- Theo Barback, 7, Cambridge

:THE FOUR SEASONS:

SUMMER:

Beams of heat radiate the animals below as the bask in the rays, many already waiting for warmth to arrive. Living the easy life, munching on the brightest green carpet and weeding the fields. The cover of the forest is dotted by glimpses of sunlight welcoming the animals to relax.

In the city families are leaving their houses to enjoy a day out at park and zoos, some will travel further for a getaway.

AUTUMN:

Autumn makes the leaves turning rainbow hues, a different colour for each leaf. When they fall, homes are made for hedgehog families all season round. Make sure you do not fall down the burrows the rabbits dig, hidden from predators by the multicoloured leaves. The owls live in the barest trees, watching the night turn to new day. Finally, the mice and rats hide away from those who seek them.

Autumn provides a shelter for all animals to make sure they stay safe.

WINTER:

In winter the birds sing an early song as the day begins. Soon they set off following the fresh winter breeze while humans and their furry companions skid across the pavements not realizing the slippery dangers.

Most stay inside huddling together but others explore the frosty wonderland. Snow ices the ground like a cake.

SPRING:

Spring is the season of new beginnings, it is when the flowers sprout their first bloom and the winter thaws away, seeping the colour back into the land. The animals are released from their hibernation as the sun awakens them from their deep slumber. April showers fall from the skies bringing new life and germination.

Springtime brings children back out to parks, enjoying the wildlife and weather. It is the season of new growth and preparation for the long summer days ahead.

- Eden Barnes, 9, Nottingham

:WOLFIE:

Wolfie has teeth like swords.

Wolfie has fur like velvet.

Wolfie has eyes like the sea.

Wolfie has ears like a mountain's peak.

Wolfie has claws like a blade of grass.

Wolfie has paws like beanbags.

Wolfie is my favourite little puppy and my perfect companion, my best buddy, the other sock from a matching pair, my little doggy, my mischief-maker.

- Eden Barnes, 9, Nottingham

:OCTOBER:

She knew Halloween was near as the nights crept in closer and closer.

As the wind blew viscously through the trees, she smelt the cold while she crashed through the crunchy leaves.

Her glasses steamed up as she sipped her hot coffee on her way home.

Soon she would be cosy in front of a roaring fire with her furry companion and she could not think of anything more pleasing.

- Niamh Barnes, 11, Antrim

:AUTUMN:

It is getting cold,
Hedgehogs are getting sleepy
Autumn is coming!

- Harvey Bartlett-Rawlings,7, Norfolk

:THE MYSTERIES OF THE ISLAND:

The ominous mist covers the remote Isle
as the looming watch towers protect it

Below, the waves crash violently
against the cliff, spraying the towers above

Craggy old huts are infused
with yellow, bright torches

As the sheep graze happily, unaware
of the danger lurking in the sky

All of a sudden, darkened beasts swiftly snatch some sheep from the
sloping hill

The darkened beasts reveal themselves
in the torch light

...

Dragons!

- Harry Charlie Bench, 9, Plymouth

:ACROSTIC MINECRAFT POEM:

Mining is one of the most important things to do

Igloos can be found in ice biomes

Never dig straight down

Evil bunnies are very rare

Crafting tables can craft anything

Rabbits like carrots

Axes chop wood faster than your fist

Fish can be found in rivers

The ocelot scares creepers

- Jacob Blockley-Walker, 11, N.E. Lincs

:SUMMER:

Sun shining here and there,
birds singing in the Summer air.
Nice and cool in the ice cold pool,
getting sprayed down by the garden hose,
cool and refreshing, I suppose.

It's hot inside they say,
so let's go outside and play on this particularly hot day.
The horses in the field go neigh,
all the children go YAY!

- Nicole Bourne, 9, Norfolk

Stripes go up
Some go down
Some go left
And some go right.
They can go anywhere!

Who am I?
Am I a fool
Or am I a pool?
Please, please,
Tell me what I am!

- Elias Jun Choi Bowers, 7, Essex

:ANGRY SEA, HAPPY SEA, BEAUTIFUL SEA:

I can see it from my window
It changes all the time
Every wave is different
Not all its moods are kind

It can be cruel and nasty
Cold and vicious too
Rough and raging temper
Angry thrashing blue

Monster in the shadows
Creatures in the dark
Beady eyes hunting
Could it be a shark

Sometimes it is happy
Sparkling in the sun
Beautiful, salty, warm
Our favourite place for fun

We love to walk on the beach
Cheeky waves tickling toes
Finding sea glass treasure
Out the tide goes

Quiet, calm, relaxing
Paddle boarding smooth
Get your board shorts on
Get into our paddle board groove

- Luca and Maximo Bradbury-Ross, 9, Felixstowe

:LEMON SHERBERTS FALL FROM THE RAIN CLOUDS ABOVE:

When lemon sherbets fall from the rain clouds up so tall

When the ball rolls down the hill to get to the shops till

When the dog gets the ball, the dog gets so tall

- Samuel Bradley, 6, Cheshire

:IF ONLY....A LITTLE POEM BY HARRISON:

If only, I could steal the clouds and turn them into the world's most comfiest chair.

If only, I could control the clocks and go into the future.

If only, I could harness the weather so I could make it cold on a hot summer's day.

If only, I could control nature and turn cities green.

If only, I had a trunk and could use it to steal all the sadness in the world.

If only, I could live forever and experience all life's greatest gifts.

- Harrison Brewer, 9, Shouldham

:THE BOTTLE:

When my Nan died It was the first time I saw Mum cry.
Just on the floor in the kitchen.
Sobbing.
I don't remember the funeral.
When we got home my Mum had a glass of wine.
The bottle in fact.
I didn't know it then but my Mum would have another tomorrow.
And another.
Mum didn't stop.
I tried to get her help. Begged her to stop.
She didn't.
I was scared. I was sad. I felt helpless.
Then Mum stopped.

- William Brodzinski, 12, Shinfield

2020, what a year,
It hasn't brought us any cheer,
We're all staying safe,
At our place
The place that we call home,
Even when you feel alone,
You are not unknown.

Just in case you're unaware,
Coronavirus isn't very fair,
These masks we must wear,
To go out, if we dare.

When other countries were locking down,
Boris said, with a frown,
Wash your hands,
So many demands, cancel your plans!

And on Thursday nights,
It was such a delight,
We'd bang our pans,
And clap our hands.

The weeks tick by,
More and more people die,
Our family, our friends,
When will this end?

From stay home, stay safe,
The mantra began to change,
Stay alert, go to work!
Control the virus, it lurks!

As lockdown started to lift,
People began to shift,
No-one knew whether it was safe,
But people went out, in any case!

Stay 2 metres apart –
it breaks my heart!
But I know in the end,
I'll be able to hug my family and friends.

- Aidan Brown, 13, Barwell (Written at age 11)

:IMPOSTER:

There's an impostor among us, only one is sus.
There's 14 safe and they all think I'm sus.
I saw red shapeshift in admin,
They also think it's Chad, he didn't sin.
I did scan and asteroids, everyone saw.
I saw red, he unhinged his jaw.

- Elijah Buckley, 10, Teesside

Though the common crow is seen as dark and dreary
There is much more to behold
Though it flies on days bleak and bleary
There is hidden grace it holds.

Its unkindness may descend upon forgotten land
And it may scavenge the ground for food
It has the remains of prey in the palm of its hand
And its methods of hunting are quite crude.

Though the crow was an omen in stories of the past
With its cry akin to a macabre hymn,
The depth of its beauty is rather vast
And maybe admiring one wouldn't be such a sin.

- **Calliope Buckley, 12, Teesside**

:AUTUMN LEAVES:

I really do like autumn,
The colours on the trees, the changes in the leaves,
Their colours alight in the autumn evening light,
Coating everything with a golden shimmering haze,
Shining on the leaves tumbling down from their trees,
Eventually dying down to a dirty brown,
Lying on the ground,
Waiting for me to crunch under my feet,
Telling us that autumn is here.

- Charlotte Chillman, 9, Newark

:NATURE AND THE SENSES:

I like to see people swimming in the lake,
I don't like to see bugs munching at my blackberries!

I love to hear waves crashing in the sea,
I really really don't like to hear the phone ring!

I smell the air, it smells refreshing,
I don't like to smell dog poos!

I like to touch blackberries as they squish in my fingers.
I don't like to touch nettles, they sting.

I love summer pears and summer plums and all the
summer fruit
The skin is furry in my mouth and the inside tastes juicy.

- Jesse Chillman, 5, Newark

:SKATEBOARDING:

Standing on my board
Keeping control of my balance
An intimidating ramp challenging me
Turning my board in a Pop Shove-It.
Excitement all over me.

- Dylan Cole-Reeve, 10, Norfolk

:FOREST FAIRIES:

Forest flowers scattered across the path
Orange, red so many colours like a sea of fire
Running and playing, fairies and children
Every fairy likes to play in the vibrant green grass
Sprinkling fairy dust to give the world a little sparkle
To spread a little happiness to all.

Fairies small enough to fit in a pocket like loose pennies
A floaty dress and flower crown
Inside a hollow tree they make their homes
Riding the river on tiny leaf boats
In flight their wings beat like tiny cymbals
Enchantingly dancing in the sunlight
Spectacular magic within the forest.

- Rose Cole-Reeve, 13, Norfolk

:AUTUMN:

A cosy night by the fire
Under a snuggly, warm blanket
Tea cup steaming
Under the leaves is a hedgehog sniffing
Multi coloured leaves, so pretty
Next is November!

- Chloe Cuzick, 9, Worcester

:THE PARK:

I love running down hills,
I see dogs run too.
Families having picnics,
their dogs have some too.

I see fairy doors,
hidden in trees.
I sit on the floor,
hoping they open their magical doors.

I laugh and play with my sister,
on the zip line, slide and swings.
We go so high we see the flowers,
and feel like we have wings.
I love going to the park and it's one of my favourite things.

:MOUSE:

Mice are cute
Oh the mouse ate the cheese
Usually the mouse eats biscuits to
Silly mouse likes my slide
Emma (mommy) loves my mouse

- Isobella Davis-Healey, 7, Birmingham

:RABBIT:

Rabbits are cute
A rabbit likes carrots
Balls are fun for Rabbits to play with
Biscuits and carrots for a rabbit
Isobella (sister) bunny
Today it is rabbit's birthday

:MY BUNNY:

I want a bunny,
to snuggle and stroke.
She would have the smallest paws,
that is no joke.

Her name would be Hopity Flopity,
she is cute, fluffy and brown.
With a chocolate button nose,
and her ears pointing down.

She would crunch her carrots,
and follow me around.
Climb up me,
and jump to the ground.
Everyone loves bunnies . . . . . I want a bunny.

- Poppy Davis-Healey, 7, Birmingham

There was a young bat,
Who was furry and fat.
Couldn't fit in his cave
So he had a shave,
And went on a diet and got flat.

There was a boy who went to the shop.
He bought a bottle of pop.
Then he went out
And he had to shout
Because he couldn't open the top.

There was a tall man
Who ran and ran and ran.
Couldn't remember
Was it because of September
Oh no, he just went to see his gran.

- Marco Drew, 8, Forest of Dean
- (Illustrations by Logan Drew, 10, Forest of Dean)

:THE OLD OAK TREE:

Hello old Oak, so big and tall
You make all the other trees,
Seem so small!
Is it your rough trunk, or rigid leaves?
Or thick branches, which hold a home for bees?
It could be your appearance, so old and wise,
Have you seen the cave men?
Or Henry the Eighth and his wives?
It could be the answers, you hold in your roots,
Like old, ancient language,
Or old, ancient books?
Maybe the facts that sit high in your branches,
Like towns and cities and villas and ranches?
Whatever's the answer, whatever's the truth,
The old Oak's amazing, and stay that, it should!

- Jess Duggan, 11, Derby

:BUMBLEBEE:

Oh, Bumblebee,
How loud and proud,
Your beautiful patterns,
And buzzing so loud,
Not a Honeybee, making sweet treats,
Not a Carpenter bee, housing in woods not your beat,
Your job is so simple, but important as well,
You pollinate flowers, you're so good as well!
You do your job, day after day after day,
Go back to the hive, sleep and then take,
Your full rested body, out all again,
And when you finally finish,
Go back to your den,
And do the same thing,
Over again!

- Jess Duggan, 11, Derby

:WHEN THE FOREST FALLS ASLEEP:

The tree yawns,
And the bird snores,
While the forest falls asleep.
Rabbits curl up,
Squirrels tails twirl up,
And the badger tucks it's baby to sleep.

- Lilly Elwardany, 7, London

:ADVENTURE IN THE SEA:

Dipping my toes in the big blue sea
I dive into my watery adventure!

Something bobbly and wobbly wiggling in the sea
It's a jellyfish! It's sneakily bobbing towards me

Something small and curious comes my way
My! It's a seahorse with all it's babies having a good day!

As I go further I see a knobbly hard shell
It's a cute little turtle that's come to see me as well!

OUCH!! Who just pinched me? Oh! It's Mister Hermit Crab!
He loves to surprise me with his pincers - it's more than just a grab!

A thick cloud of ink surrounds my hand,
I turn to see an octopus in the sea floor sand!

Suddenly a large set of teeth come near,
It's a shark! Help! He's almost here!

I think my adventure must now end
While each of the fish is still my friend!

- Lilly Elwardany, 7, London

:BRITISH GREYS:

Supermarket neon, chip shop blues.
Short days, early nights and mid-winter flues.
Jaunts to Grandmother's house, far-away places
Looking at your beat-up shoes, doing up the laces.
Preparing for Christmas in December,
even though Christ was born in September
What a dingy dining room philosophy.
Everyone's so sad it's nearly a comedy.
Talking to the moon, talking to Selene,
and complaining, today, the world just feels so mean.
McDonalds coffee, midnight drives.
Staring out at other peoples' little lives.
Early evening games of kids playing football.
Little kid called Jacob scores a goal.
Community centre yellow lighting.
Disadvantaged youths, in a park fighting.
British weather, British greys.
British sadness, people stuck in their ways.

- Eva Firnigl, 14, Tyne and Wear

:FUN IN THE SUN:

Fun in a field is a festival,
Farm animals roam free.

Benji and I were in a dog show!
There were fun games too,
Hit the tree, win a teddy.
Superhero, superhero - India, come play with me!

I am going home now,
Tired, sweaty and happy.

(Benji is my dog. India is my cousin and best friend)

- Luke Freemantle, 8, Ogbourne St George

:DOGS:

Dogs are full of love and cuddles,
When there are lots, you can call it a puppy puddle.

He will sit with you his tail wagging,
But not for long, soon he will be zig zagging!

Then at night he will snuggle up,
And you will tell him he has been a good pup.

- Mya Freemantle, 12, Ogbourne St George

:PUGS!:

Pugs are cute.
Unnecessary for them to look like they've got hit in the face with a
frying pan
Good that they've got tiny and floppy ears and cute faces.

- Stanley Galloway, 9, Darlington

:HALLOWEEN:

Heart stopping shrieks echo

All across the land

Late at night

Luring, loathsome, lily-livered

Ogres bash and brawl while growling and scowling

Werewolves prowl with

Eerie howls

Entombed evil rises

Nightmares of the nighttime are here

- Grace Gannon, 14, Teesside

:SNUGGLES IN BED:

I snuggle in bed with my mummy
And my daddy
(Well I used to)
It makes me feel happy in my tummy
Yes yes in my tummy

- Raven Rain Gaskin, 5, Derby

:CHRISTMAS DAY:

Snow has freshly fallen.
Not a footprint to be seen.
Icicles are dropping to join in with the scene.

Cats are waking up, hear their soft little purrs.
Birds are chirping a Christmas tune, presents will be opened soon.
What a fun day, now it's time to go and sleigh.

:MAGIC OF NATURE:

Grass is talking
Leaves are walking
Trees are snorting

- Hayley Gerber, 7, Norfolk

:FUN:

The sun is shining, everyone is going out to play. Nothing is going to stop us today!

- Robyn Gerber, 5, Norfolk

:THE FROG CALLED POG:

There once was a frog called Pog
Who loved to swim in the Bog.
One day he met a dog,
"Hi, I'm Gog" said the dog.
Then suddenly, out of the fog
Came a giant rolling log.
A boy called Cog, he stopped the log
And threw it into the bog.

- Caleb Oliver Grant (aka COG), 9, Histon

:FELICITY THE FAUN:

There was a little faun
Her name was Felicity
She loved to fight other fauns
And she loved to solve mysteries
Felicity had a dream:
To fly in the sky!
One day she asked bee
"How do you fly high?"
Bee was confused!
"You can't fly, you're a faun!
You've got four legs
You only stand on the lawn!"
Felicity was sad,
Her head drooped down,
Tears fell from her eyes,
On her head was a frown.
Then, in a flash of light,
A wizard came by!
And he magicked Felicity
So she could fly!
She glided through the air,
With excitement and delight
She felt like she was flying
Just like a kite!
Felicity's dream
It came true!
And just like hers
Yours can too!

- Iris Grant, 5, Histon

58

:AURORA BOREALIS:

The northern lights,
Higher than kites.
The lovely pink,
Just as I blink.
I see a crow,
Does he feel the colourful flow?

- Alex H, 12, Saltburn-By-The-Sea

:WINTER POND:

The pond was frozen
The ducks were sliding on ice
Frogs hibernating

- Olivia H, 8, Saltburn-By-The-Sea

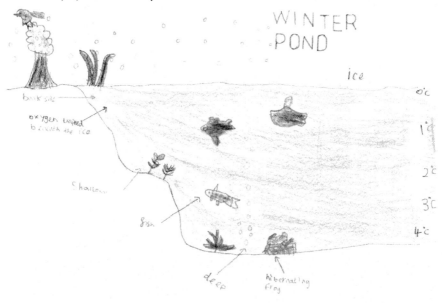

:MY WASP POEM:

Wasps Can live in Germany,
They like to scavenge for lunch,
They fly about all day long,
To find there next big munch.

European wasps are aggressive,
And are attracted to sugary drinks,
They hibernate in the winter,
And sometimes give you a wink.

Flying high all day long,
I'm getting really tired,
Dodging soap and water,
I'm feeling quite inspired.

I use my antenna to see,
And my wings fall down when I rest,
I build my home in sheltered places,
I love my family nest.

- Millie-Ray Halpin, 10, Cropwell Bishop

:OREO:

Oreo is a worm,
He wiggles really slow
A bird took him for her dinner,
But then dropped him down below

:ANTS:

Ants are always busy
Nest building and collecting food.
They always work together

- Owl Halpin, 5, Cropwell Bishop

:PERFECT PUFFINS:

Puffins fly all through the day,

Under the ground the little ones play,

For the Puffling time does fly, watching its Mummy fly through the sky

From up high Mummy puffin can see her nest

In the hole of her home she can see her Puffling having a rest

Now we have made a puffin friend, it is time for this poem to end

- Evelyn Hardy, 10, Edwinstowe

:I LOVE CHICKENS:

Chickens can peck and be quite flappy,
But they always make me happy.
All chickens dig and all of them preen,
Some even lay special eggs that are green.
Some are big and some are small,
And they know I love them all.

- Keira Hardy, 11, Edwinstowe

:WISE OWL:

Owl glides and owl swoops
In the dark
A wise flying creature, finding a feast
In the dark.

:A HAIKU - PRETTY SNOWFLAKE:

Pretty little snowflake
Its pattern so elegant
Oh what beauty winter brings.

- **Eve Harris, 8, Millisle**

:TRANSFORMER:

Car, car
Drive, drive
Open doors, shut doors
Open bonnet, shut bonnet
Open boot, shut boot
Wings spread wide
Wheels spin
As it drives along the road

:A BUNCH OF STUFF IN THE LIVING ROOM:

Yellow flashes
Red flashes
Pink flashes
Heart pink flashes
Barn doors open and shut
Cup holders flash
Silver nobbles, gold nobbles on flags
Music notes dance along the lines
Indie is a blanket

- Indie Hartland, 6, Guisborough

:THE PRINCESS OF THE DARK:

In the night some people have a fright but not the princess of the dark.

She Gallops around like a merry-go-round.

She stares at the stars wondering if she will ever see Mars.

One day when she floated in space, she glanced on a river of milk that looked a little like silk.

Colours twirl, planets spin, stars glide within; make a wish on a shooting star it will take you very far.

A little bit of dust and rock, a pinch of hydrogen and waterto fill it up, to make a planet not too cold but not too hot.

I live in the galaxy, I sleep in the day, I play in the dark.

You might wonder why Space is called Space when the atmosphere is so light, or earth can go dark while the galaxy stars are so bright.

Have you ever seen Saturn with it's ring of stone or my jewels orbiting the stars?

Even my crown disperses and loses its weight, when the gravity isn't as great

and so, this my loyal subjects, has been the grand debate.

- Asiyah Alice Hassane, 7, London

:MY SECRET GARDEN:

There is somewhere in this world
I know there is somewhere
I sit there on the grass
In the summer air
A cool clear stream runs through the grass
Where little fish swim
The water looks like shimmering glass
Poppies and primroses grow upon the grass
Daisies and butter cups spring up everywhere!
Rabbits bounce across I am still when they pass
Little birds singing their evening song
The shadows are getting long
I think it's time for dinner I should be getting home
I love my secret garden I will come back every
DAY
Me & the birds & the bunnies will come back to
play.

- Jessica Anne Hatt, 8, Windsor

:OUR PETS:

Our Hens

Our hens are bantams
They are very small
And they are definitely not very tall
They like sweetcorn
But they can't move a pawn
Over a chess board of wood
But they could have a bath in the mud.

Our Budgies

Our budgies are blue
and green
their water is clean
and they like to preen.

Our Canaries

Our canaries like millet
but I've never seen them spill it
they like cuttlebone
and I've never heard them moan.

- Aazer Hirst-Khadir, 10, Grimsby

:THE ODYSSEY:

Odysseus's odyssey
Does go on adventures. Do
You like tales of
Sea monsters?
Scary cyclopes?
Even Gods? Then
You'll like the Odyssey.

- Aazer Hirst-Khadir, 10, Grimsby

:MY CHICKENS:

Chicky likes black seeds.

The chicken house is for all the chickens.

Rainbow ate a black seed that Chicky really wanted to eat.

- Musa Hirst-Khadir, 4, Grimsby

:DINOSAURS:

Dinosaurs! T-Rex bit other dinosaurs.

Iguanodon was the second dinosaur to be named – in 1825

Nearby volcanoes erupted.

Omnivores, carnivores, herbivores

Some dinosaurs ate meat, some dinosaurs ate plants and some dinosaurs ate both.

Ankylosaurus is my favourite because of the tail club.

Up high brachiosaurus ate plants – they had a long neck.

Raptors ate meat.

Stegosaurus had plates

- Salar Hirst-Khadir, 6, Grimsby

:SAVE THE ENVIRONMENT:

Save the environment
from hunters, loggers, air pollution.
Get together with your friends
and start a revolution.

To help save the environment
you can just do something small,
here are some things you can do at home,
You or anyone at all:

Put bird feeders in your garden,
Eat less meat.
Plant flowers for bees and butterflies
In rows pretty and neat,

Grow some of your own food,
Use less plastic,
Find ways to save water.
These changes could be drastic.

Instead of going in your cars
Why not walk or cycle?
Pick up litter that you see
And remember: always recycle

- Shuky Hirst-Khadir, 12, Grimsby

:GREEK GODS RAP:

Zeus
Married to Hera,
Zeus the almighty
Led the defeat of the Titans
Rules Olympia rightly.

Hera
Queen of the Gods,
Zeus's wife.
Hates his affairs
And ruins their life

Poseidon
Brother of Zeus,
God of the sea
All earthquakes
Are controlled by he.

Hades
Brother of Zeus,
God of the underworld
If you're good: Elysium.
If not, into Tartarus you'll be hurled.

Athena
Goddess of wisdom,
Goddess of warfare.
If she picks a side
Then the war won't be fair.

Dionysus
Born from Zeus's thigh,
God of ecstasy and wine
Had lots of followers
who were drunk most of the time.

Apollo
God of music and healing,
God of light
Twin brother of
The Goddess of the night.

Artemis
Animals' huntress and protector,
Goddess of the night.
Twin sister of
The God of music, healing and light.

Hermes
Messenger of the Gods,
Stole cattle minutes after he was born.
Invented the first lyre
Winged helmet and sandals he's worn.

Aphrodite
Goddess of love,
Born from sea foam.
Aphrodite in Greece,
And Venus in Rome.

Ares
Ares, he's
The god of war:
Out on the battlefield
With all the blood and gore.

Demeter
Goddess of the harvest,
Persephone's mother,
Had 2 children to her brother Zeus:
Iacchus is the other.

Hephaestus
Hephaestus the blacksmith God
He made weapons for battle.
He also made Heracles
A Stymphalian bird-scaring rattle.

Hestia
Goddess of the hearth,
Zeus's sister
Goddess of home:
Her name's Hestia.

- Shuky Hirst-Khadir, 12, Grimsby

:MARIO VS WARIO:

It's-a me Mario
my brother is Luigi
I am a plumber
I will destroy the Koopalings and-a Bowser Jr and-a Bowser!

ioıɹɐɯ ʎoɹʇsǝp ll!ʍ ı
ʎǝuoɯ ʇuɐʍ ı
ıɓınlɐʍ sı ɹǝɥʇoɹq ʎɯ
oıɹɐʍ ǝɯ ɐ-s,ʇı

:BUDGIE RAP ACROSTIC:

I have 2 budgies called Flash and Ice.

Flash is cute. He
Likes chewing cardboard
And eating seeds.
So fast-
He goes side to side.

Ice is blue. She
Can dance. She likes
Eating millet.

- Yuunis Hirst-Khadir, 8, Grimsby

:ALL ABOUT ME:

I am a strong little girl
Who loves to sing and dance
And do archery

I am strong little girl
Who really loves cupcakes
I love to bake them with my mum

I am a strong little girl
I love to go out and play

I am a strong little girl
Who likes the animal world
I love to go play with my pet bunny.

I am a strong little girl
Who likes to laugh and twirl
I'd like to learn the trapeze

I am a strong little girl
And I like to read

I am a strong little girl
My favourite colours are all shades of purple
My favourite animal is a bunny

I am a strong little girl
My favourite person in history is Boudicca
My favourite pokemon are eevee and lunarla

I am a strong little girl
I like to listen to music with my mum
We dance and sing along

I am a strong little girl
I like to go on night walks

- FISH POO! -

Fish poo fish poo
It really is the worst
Don't drink it, don't sniff it
It really is the worst!

- Tiffany Horton, 7, Wiltshire

:THE CLOCK, THE FOX AND THE LOCK:

Once there was a clock who had a lock and on that lock, there was a box
And in that box, there was a fox.
And on that fox, there was lots of locks.
And on those locks, there was lots of clocks.

:THE MOLE, BULB AND THE BOWL:

Once there was a bulb,
who sat on a mole,
who had a bowl in its hole
And the bowl had a hole.

'Oh no!' Says the mole
'Bulb?'
'Will you buy me a new bowl?'
'Yes' says Bulb
'STUPENDOUS!' shouts the mole

- Toby Horton, 11, Wiltshire

:ODE TO MY OLD, EAST-END AUNT:

There was an old lady who came from East London
I don't know why she came from East London
She came from East London and married a man
I don't know why she married a man
She married a man and had two boys
I don't know why she had two boys...
She just did.

There was an old lady who came from East London
I don't know why she came from East London
She came from East London and married a man
I don't know why she married a man
She married a man and had two boys
I don't know why she had two boys...
She had a young nephew who was her favourite
I don't know why he was her favourite...
He just was.

There was an old lady who had a full life
She came from East London and married a man
She had two boys and a favourite nephew
But then something sad happened...her husband died
She lived for years and years and years
But then ... she also, sadly died.

I think of her life, full of great memories
And I just smile.

- George Hurd, 12, Barnard Castle

:ADHD:

ADHD, buzzing like a bee,
But I don't want to get up in the morning.
Ants in my pants, hurricane in my brain,
And sitting still is BORING!

Talking like a racing car at one hundred miles an hour,
Forgetting what I'm doing in the middle of a shower!
Headaches from life, like a firefly at night,
Drawn to mischief like a moth to the light!

ADHD, feel frustrated at me,
The bouncy ball inside makes me angry.
Calm can't be found, can't concentrate on me,
Never mind anyone else that's around.

But when I find something I REALLY like,
You had better strap in and hold on tight.
My superpower lights a fire inside,
And I won't stop learning until I reach the sky!

- Harmonie-Rose Husk, 6, Essex

:RAINFOREST:

Raindrops splash
And parrots chatter
In the understory fruit bats flutter.
Noisy monkeys swing through the trees
Forest floor is full of jaguars and leaves.
Ocelots, hummingbirds, tigers, sloths
Rustling, scuttling, clammy and hot
Enormous tarantulas, scorpions hissing,
Slithering snakes, trees burned and missing
Toucans, frogs, butterflies and ants

We have to help the animals however we can!

- Harmonie-Rose Husk, 6, Essex

:THE END OF THE WORLD:

When I woke up this morning I never imagined today would be the end of the world!
The grey, stormy sky looked suspiciously dry, but the dark clouds made the air feel cold.

I felt the ground shake, was it an earthquake? Then a rumble was heard far away.
The rumble grew louder, the pictures fell down, and I didn't feel safe to stay.

Outside the cracks opened, volcanoes erupted with fireworks of orange and gold.
The sky was alight with lightning so bright, and we no longer feared the cold.

The cracks were so deep, the people just screamed, as I stood shaking with fear,
The houses on fire, flames higher and higher, and our destiny became clear.

The wind roared past, aggressively fast,
It hurt my ears it was so loud,
Destroying trees and cars and anything in its path, swirling round and round with a howl.

The wind died down, and ashes fell creating a crown of grey on the ground,
I was no longer choking on the smell of smoke, but our town could no longer be found.

Then the rain came, acting exactly the same, battering everything down below
The floods sailed high, right up to the sky, and we no longer had a home.

- Melodie-Eve Husk, 11, Essex

:TIGERS:

Tigers are orange and have long claws,
In the jungle they walk on all fours,
Going to hunt birds and Monkeys
Everyday any animal he sees
Roaring, pouncing, creeping and waiting
Scared little animals fear and hate him.

:RAINFOREST:

Rustling Monkeys swinging through the trees
And slithering snakes and buzzy bees
In the forest floor it is dark, damp and humid
Noisy, deadly, awake, busy,
Floral, leafy, rainy, and bright
Orangutans swinging and bats at flight
Rotting trees and fast running rivers
Everywhere flapping from brightly coloured beaks and feathers
Springy frogs and lazy sloths
Towering high like the butterflies and moths.

- Melodie-Eve Husk, 11, Essex

:WE WAIT:

We watch as the trees age
We watch, we watch, we wait
We listen to the sad song of the leaves
We listen, we listen, we wait
We feel the scarred edges of the bark
We feel, we feel, we wait
We are one with the trees
We forget, we forget
Yet the trees are one with us,
Remember

- Arthur Hutchinson, 9, High Peak

:THE DIFFERENT MONSTER:

Creeping through the wet, wild wood
Hiding in the bushes
Was a shy, different kind of monster
Looking for a friend
Covered in leaf and river coloured scales
With shiny, curved horns upon its head
Eyes as wide and as bright as the stars
Our shy monster met a new friend

Along came a family walking through the wood
Out crept the monster from its leafy bush
"Hello" the monster said in a quiet sort of way
"Argh" shrieked the parents running fast away
The child stayed still
Raised its hand and waved
Happily the pair went off
Into the woods to play

- Dottie Hutchinson, 6, High Peak

:TRICK OR TREAT:

It's the dead of night
All the children are asleep
But no one has turned off the light

The bare trees shiver
Wolves howl at the moon
Spirits run free

"Open" a door creaks
And in the doorway stands
A witch, a zombie and a ghostie

If you look closely
They're not what they seem
Just some face paint
A black hat and an old white sheet

Little monsters
Big smiles on their faces
Wandering the cobbled streets

Trick or treat they shout
For it is Halloween

- Tilly Hutchinson, 11, High Peak

:AUTUMN WONDERS:

The Autumn leaves fall from the trees
As golden as can be
They said to each other, as the wind blew them on an adventure
"I wonder where we'll be."

Whoosh! Over the hills they flew
"Duck!" they cried, as they went under human legs
"Turn!" they shouted, as they nearly crashed into trees
Then they came to a stop in a soft, lush garden
"So this is where we'll be"

- Saaliha Jackson, 8, London

:EARTH SLEEPS:

The moon shone brightly in the sky
It looked down at the Earth and said,
"Rest your sleepy head, let your dreams flow.
When you're asleep I will protect you from the night.
Now day is coming, I must go
But don't worry, I'll be back tomorrow."

- Zahra Jackson, 7, London

:FLAT WHITE BOTTOM BUMPER FUN!:

I skiddy down the hall
Into the bathroom,
The flat white bottom bumper was polished
I plopped myself down
Its very cold,
I hold my white bottom wipers and heaved,
A ploppy plop came out,
The wiff woff was hideous,
I wiped my botty butt,
Then I pushed the cracker button hard down and washed my handy-
hands,
My red flat dryer was wet,
So I bottom bashed them dry instead.

- Anna Johnson, 8, Birmingham

:1:

Hey, I'm on a boat in the middle of the sea,
Three seagulls fly past and a Viking behind me.
The waves are so splashy like in a big storm,
So I go under deck, so it's still warm.

:2:

Apples in autumn,
Apples so red,
Apples, yes apples,
Just right for my ted.

- Alina Jones, 7, Walthamstow

:NIBBLES:

Never before
I've loved someone more...
Burrowing in bedding, as you do in my heart.
Bathing in sand
Like you own the land
Every time you make me laugh
Surprising me everyday

- Leya-Rose Jones, 12, Chester

:BEAUTY CAN'T BE CAPTURED:

When you see something beautiful
That makes you stop and stare
you might pick up your phone
And get a picture of what is there

When you look at that photo
you may see a pretty scene
it will have captured some beauty
But not all that you had seen

You can't capture anything
with as good quality as your eyesight
the details never even look close
To how they do in real life

You can't capture the night
or the glittering white stars
nor the circular glowing moon
all of this is only visible in your sight

You can't capture the sun
In any photo it is shamed
it becomes more of a dull sparkle
And it only has pale-coloured rays

You can't capture the beach
or the sparkly waves
and yellow sand is simply that
it's no longer a place where
anyone would want to relax

Whilst you can capture
Emotions of people
you don't see what made them smile
or how they stayed that way for a while

you can't capture
how special a moment can be
the detail in any photo
Can then be disappointing to see

you can't capture
How pretty people look
Only the distorted image of them
in the photo you took

there are many more reasons
why beauty isn't always seen
but it is important to understand
that beauty can't accurately be shown on any screen

- Summer Jones, 14, Barnard Castle

:THE RESCUE DOG:

I awaited the surprise
The minutes took what felt like years to pass by
As I wondered to myself
What is this surprise?

Finally it was ready
I ran down the stairs
And there a saw a puppy
Eating every scrap of food from her bowl

She didn't look the same
As the other dogs
Her skin was loose on her
And her ears flopped

But I loved her
From the day I saw her
And I couldn't wait
To care for her

And every walk
Or cuddle we've shared
Has been so comforting

Even though I'm not perfect
And neither is she
We get along perfectly
Just her and me

They say "get a rescue dog" it could save their life
And I may have saved hers
But also, She saved mine.

- Summer Jones, 14, Barnard Castle

:THE WISHING WELL:

Make a wish at the dish
in the wishing well.
Make a wish in the wishing well.
Make a wish in the wishing-wishing well
at the dish, but please don't tell.

The hairy fairy is really scary.
So close your eyes, don't tell lies
in disguise and throw a boingy coin in.
Otherwise the hairy fairy will come.
The hairy fairy will come.

Make a wish at the dish
in the wishing well.
Make a wish in the wishing well.
Make a wish in the wishing-wishing well
at the dish, but please don't tell.

- Phoebe Kelly-Jack, 8, Broxbourne

:TREES:

When I see a big tree I can see its whole lifetime in front of me.
 I can see the way it flows and I can see the way the branches grow.
Roots digging into the earth, as the tree grows it brings new
birth. Humans disrupting nature's cycle, cutting down trees and they
never recycle.
Can we revive what used to thrive? Humans not thinking they
cutting as an excuse just to survive.

                                      I like to climb all the way to the top to
see thousands of other trees. Feels free, feels peaceful, feels
relaxing, I feel connected to nature.
Sad to see humans cutting down what is meant to be, my generation
will fix what we want to see.
But to change the world it has to start with me.

- Raphael Kneller, 10, London

:TO BE HAPPY:

To be happy
is to love yourself.
Confidence, bravery,
without any help.
To reach and shout
I'm liked, I'm loved
I am everything I am
out,
in, out, through, and about.
To be happy is free,
and when you're happy,
to believe.

- Stella Koenig, 11, London

:ROSEBLOOM ROSES:

When the vines spread,
Seed by seed,
The colour of red,
Grows beneath.
First comes a small, leaf like twig,
Then comes the colour
That we seek within.
These are the roses that grow every year,
From vines and seeds that
spread with cheer.
These are the roses that some people call
Rosebloom roses
That make joy for us all.

- Stella Koenig, 11, London

:FLAME:

My fierce, fiery friend
You still blaze, charge and devour
Never fading flame

- Augustine Kwon, 9, London

:BONFIRE NIGHT:

Big firework show
Outside, in the dark
Noisy and colourful
Fizz, whizz, pop BANG!
In the sky
Remember remember
Explode!
Night-time
I love fireworks!
Guy Fawkes
Happy and excited
Tasty treats

- Sophia Lane, 7, Kings Lynn

:THE YEAR OF THE PUMPKIN:

Spring -
It started with a seed
A sprout started to grow
Summer -
It is now a lovely plant
With leaves creeping, flowers blooming
Grow, Grow, Grow
Autumn -
The pumpkin is ready now
It's round and bright orange
Ripe for carving
Now it has a crooked smile
Winter -
The pumpkin is alone in the deep snow
Slowly rotting away
No-one notices it
All that is left is wrinkled skin and stem.

That is the life of a pumpkin.

- Sebastian Le Mesurier, 7, Medbourne

:THE BIRD OF PREY:

It was flying through the sky
Like a Red Arrow on show
I looked and said, 'Oh my!'
As it swooped up high, down low.

My heart melted at the sight
As it dipped and dived and soared
And just seeing the bird in flight
Meant that I was never bored.

It flew through a cloud
As it swept so gracefully
And its cry shrieked long and loud
As it rang across the valley.

I had read a book about
This bird and its long flight
And I say this without a doubt
The bird was a Red Kite!

- Thomas Le Mesurier, 11, Medbourne

:MEN AT WORK:

They're digging up the road
It's getting very clear
They're digging up the road
You can hear them from here
They're digging up the road
There are workers young and old
They're digging up the road
I'm sad as it's so cold

- Thomas Le Mesurier, 11, Medbourne

:GOLDEN LIGHT:

As I swam in the river
Through the trees I caught a glimpse
Of the Sun rising
And spreading its golden light
Across the world

- Alia Longhurst-Hills, 9, Worthing

:FOREST:

Deep shade stripes the ground
The soft scent of a wild stream
Drifts through the forest

:ROSES:

Rose-scent lingers here
Fallen petals cling to earth
Though they should ascend

:OCEAN:

White horse in the foam
Flying free with the current
A seashell blessing

- Siri Longhurst-Hills, 14, Worthing

:AUTUMN WALK:

Our autumn walk today.
The sun was glistening through the golden trees.
The leaves were blowing in the breeze.

The leafy floor was very damp,
The acorns crunched beneath our feet.

I collected crunchy sticks and autumn leaves that were orange, red,
green and brown.
There were lots of leaves falling to the ground.

:ACORNS:

All around us
Crunchy leaves
Over the hill
Rocks to climb
Nuts in the trees

- Arlo Blue Maguire, 7, Nottinghamshire

:AUTUMN:

All around and everywhere you look leaves are slowly
        falling to the ground beneath your feet. The
        beautiful colours crunch as you slowly make your
        way.
Under the clear stary night skies, you lay quietly
        watching the moon slowly making its way across
        the sky.
Tomorrow is Halloween, its time to carve pumpkins,
        decorate the house and watch movies.
Unique pumpkin carvings made with your friends and
        family, lighting them up at night.
Morning light is coming later, the darkness of the night
        is creeping closer and closer as the days go on.
Now all the leaves have changed there are rivers of
        colour on the floor in front of you.

- Eadie Bea Maguire, 14, Nottinghamshire

:HARVEST MOON:

How often does the harvest moon come?
Autumn's first full moon is the harvest moon.
Ready to hibernate the animals collect seeds for winter.
Very big the moon shines down on to the world.
Every three years the moon is in October.
Second by second the moon rises.
The moon glows a bright orange colour.

Many people sit out to watch the moon.
One October evening the moon will rise.
Only some animals leave for the winter.
Not all animals will hibernate.

- Eadie Bea Maguire, 14, Nottinghamshire

:AUTUMN:

Berries are falling down below
and the wind is breezy.

Mushrooms are growing in the forest
and the ground feels damp.

The leaves are crunching under our feet
and the twigs are snapping as we walk.

Night and day the wind swirls about
and the leaves scatter to the ground.

Squirrels are collecting nuts from in the forest and they will bury
them until winter.

Squirrels will crunch acorns when it's very cold.

:SNAILS:

Snails like the rain.
Never go out in the sun, they hide in their shells and make a slime
door.
Always find them in damp places.
In the darkness they hunt.
Leave slime trails on plants.

- Oryn Hazel Maguire, 5, Nottinghamshire

:WINTER:

I shuffled out of my bedroom
I crept down the stairs
I strode through the kitchen
and I strolled through the living room
and into the garden
shocked I sobbed where is all the sun
I wailed where is all the fun
I whimpered and I wept what season has begun
then I realised the way I responded was wrong
I reflected back on the summer
then I observed
and I stared and I spied and I studied
and then I realised it was winter
summer has set off it sprinted
it dashed it drove now winter is here

- Hifzah Mahmood, 9, Birmingham

:THE SEASONS:

The beam of the light
The rays of the sun
Whatever could
Be more fun

Whenever the wind
Blows in your face
The world will turn around
And everything will say
How much, the plants grow
And the trees of course
As you know
Even though
Sometimes it's easy
To make things wrong
And get quite sneezy
But then,
I see the world is quite new
Same with me
And the tree falls
Into autumn
And the wind calls
That winter will come
And it did!

So now you know
You may be in the sun
And you may be in the snow.

- Rafaella Markham, 5, Chigwell

:THE WIND:

Once there was a somebody
A somebody who no-one knows who.
He went on a boat and met his crew.

The wind began to shake and RUMBLE then the boat began to
tumble!!!!!!!

The storm was big, then the boat began to jig.

Then it tipped over!!

- Ruben Markham, 6, Chigwell

:THE SONGS IN SPACE:

Songs in space you can't erase
For all of time
Will raise you with a ray of sunshine
And a drop of love
My lover I travel far from trade winds
I travel for you my dear
However far however near
Always for you my dear

- Ahlehgra-Neroli Mattherson, 11, Nottinghamshire

:I SIT:

I sit by the frozen streams
And I think of the holly leaves
I think sitting by the fireplace
I see red and yellow leaves
I see the frozen windows
And when the night comes
I knew something was wrong
The lights went out
My parents lit a match
The match went out
I woke before the sun was up

- Santino Mattherson, 9, Nottinghamshire

:OCEANS DEEP:

Wouldn't it be nice
To go out to sea
And swim in the oceans deep
There will be no need for sleep
So don't be counting sheep
Just swim with a great leap
See the fishes how they play
See the octopus going about his day
Watch the sea turtle in the coral
Watch the shark teaching his moral
Observe the crab with his crushing claws
Observe the dolphin moving without a pause
The oceans deep with its wonder so vast
Wants me to take it slow not fast

- Tiano Mattherson, 13, Nottinghamshire

:AUTUMN DAYS:

A golden sunset shines like a new penny.
The blue sea sky
got dark early and made
cold, wet, damp drizzly nights.
Crispy, crunchy, crackly leaves
rustled like a bell.
The skeletal tree
had a long spine like a pencil
and green frizzy hair.
Winds howled a cold breeze.
The warm hug of summer loosens its grip.
A quiet whisper in the air approaches.
Red and gold,
playful leaves on the ground
were as pretty as diamonds and jewels.
The heart of Autumn embraces itself around us.

- William McCauley-Tinniswood, 8, Greater London

:THE SCARY LABYRINTH:

A black, dark cage was surrounding me.
Glass and metal were as big as the Atlantic Ocean.
Golden neon lights flashed and flickered.
Dirt filled the city as black as mud.
Smoke took over the world with the smell of fumes
lingering in the air.
The tall disgusting blocks loomed over me.
The smoke shielded the sun.
Noises on the platform were as loud as an elephant.
Rats scuttled along the filthy cobbled pavements,
looking for crumbs dropped by pigeons
and passers-by.
I felt the wet, soggy, concrete beneath my feet.
Pavements crumbled and cracked
with dust filled jagged holes.
I could taste the smoke on my tongue.
These metal monsters roared at me.
With yellow lanterns at the front -
red fiery eyes at the back.
The city was a terrifying labyrinth to a cat.

- William McCauley-Tinniswood, 8, Greater London

:WEATHER:

The rain is bad
It's making me sad,
Every drop
Makes me flop.

The sun shines
On the good times,
A sunny day
Is a funny day.

Winter's cold
You've been told,
So wrap up tight
Because snow is in sight.

A storm in a city
What a pity,
But just sit tight
And you'll be alright.

- Jasmine Mclauchlan, 9, Desborough

:FEELING GREAT!:

Exercise is so much fun,
Especially out in the sun!

When you fall off a beam,
You'll always know, there's a cheering team!

When you're playing tennis,
Don't be a menace!

When you're tired, have a think,
You really need to have a drink!

If you play basketball
You don't have to be big or small,
Because you're the one with the ball!

- Jasmine Mclauchlan, 9, Desborough

:ANIMALS:

Animals grow in a different shape and size,
and they need our help to survive.
As weather gets hotter icebergs are melting,
on this planet we call Earth,
We need your help mending.
Endangered species like the red wolf and the red panda.
We need your help saving them and I hope there's no drama.

:THE BEST BITS ABOUT DOGS!:

Dogs are cute, especially in the sun,
They're never mute, but they're lots of fun!

They're big and small but that's not all,
They're crazy and calm,
And some wrap up to your arm!

Dogs may bark at strangers,
But really there's no danger.
Some are fluffy, some are not,
But the fluffy ones get really hot!

They're always there
Because they care.
Man's best friend,
I wish it never ends!

- Ruby Mclauchlan, 8, Desborough

:THREE TROLLS:

Once there were three trolls
In the night
They were currently stone
Until, from some miracle
A meteorite came flying from the sky
It looked like an eye
Once it hit between the trolls
It broke through the stone
And all the trolls came back to skin
And said "Confound you, wizard!"

:LIONS:

Lions, Lions, Lions
Lions are loud
Lions are yellow
Lions are proud

:POLAR BEARS:

Polar bears need the utmost care
Their thick fur, it's so unfair
They need it cold out there
But now it's burning
They'll die out there
Those cute, furry polar bears

- Xander Middlemiss, 9, Duvall, WA, USA

:ELEMENTS:

Water, fire, air & earth
Water, fire, air & earth
Water keeps us hydrated
Fire keeps us warm
Air keeps us alive
And Earth makes our home
Together we are friends
That's why we celebrate

:THE MOON:

You watch over us at night
And when light
You make the darkness, night
Light
You keep the sky bright

- Zoë Middlemiss, 11, Duvall, WA, USA

:FROM THE MIND OF A 13-YEAR-OLD GIRL:

I need a phone, I want a phone...really really bad,
And if I don't get one soon I will be really really sad.
One of the reasons I want one so bad is to talk to all my friends
And not have to ask my mum if I can have a shot of her phone.

:THE AUTUMN TREE:

The tree began to sway before
The snow begins to fill the floor
The leaves fall coloured orange and red before we all head to bed.

- Maddison Milne-Emslie, 13

There's a barrier, it leads to the water,

James tried to stop but he wasn't there on time.

"STOP," said his driver as he fell out of the cab.

He fell out.

James crashed.

The alarm is ringing, and Douglas appeared to help him.

James has got passengers

James was very happy.

Someone's coming.

Henry's coming, he is going too fast, he can't stop.

His driver applied the brakes as hard as he could.

Oh no Henry couldn't stop.

"I'm on James's branch line"

"Help"

"Stop!"

Ruben Milne-Emslie, 6

:I LOVE MY TRAINS:

A frightened thought for James and Edward and Percy too,
Gordon and the famous visitor.
James' wheels spinning and he is collecting troublesome trucks,
His wheels can't stop.
Gordon saw the commotion,
James slid into the station,
James sped past Henry.
He is on the branch line.
"Stop"
"Oh no"
"I can't stop.

Ruben Milne-Emslie, 6

:VOLCANO:

Volcano still and quiet
Pressure builds
Heat rises
Angry Volcano
Danger, eruption
Ash, lava
Calm again.

- Lucy-Kate Myers-Lowe, 9, Birmingham

:ROBOT PENGUINS:

The robot penguins were terrorizing the streets.
Looking for delicious, stinky, fishy treats.
The supermarket was invaded by a horde of them.
They found the fish aisle - more precious to them than a shiny gem.
Another group of penguins had invaded the school.
The schoolchildren said "Robot penguins! So cool!"
The town mayor was in a lot of distress.
He called animal control to clean up the mess.
The men had cold ruthless looks in their eyes.
Their boss said "Come on! Let's exterminate them guys!"
Their nets caught all the penguins, one by one.
The men cheered as the boss said "Today is a penguin free eon!"
But the penguins were *robot* penguins and they fired laser beams
out of their eyes.
All the exterminators were taken by surprise.
Their feet turned into rocket boosters and they zoomed into the sky.
"We let them all escape." Said the boss with a sigh.
The penguins zoomed off to the moon.
But just you wait, they'll come back to earth soon.
Eon — a long period of time, a word included in this rhyme.

- Johan Oosthuizen, 12, Londonderry

:GREEDY, NASTY, GERTRUDE:

Once, there was a greedy girl called Gertrude,
And she indeed, was very rude
She bossed her parents all the time
Making them clean the dirt and slime
Se treated them like her personal slaves
She had suitable punishments like shutting them up in deep dark caves,
Or making them eat disgusting worm-infested stinky cheese,
Mashed up with rotten foul-smelling peas.
For breakfast, this foul creature's parents had,
Something that tasted, smelt and looked bad
This is what they made for themselves
They just got any scraps left on the shelves,
A vomited banana, a thousand years old
A half-eaten brussel sprout (*For them, this was like finding 24-carat gold*)
Gertrude, meanwhile had the breakfast of a millionaire
Ice-cream pizza and jelly-bean cake (*Which she would never share*)
But how did she make her parents do what she ordered?
Well Gertrude had been born with a condition
Called ELSD but her parents had a superstition
That their baby got her loud voice from the nurses screaming
(*ELSD stands for Extremely Loud Screaming even when you're Dreaming*)
Her voice could make your eardrums burst and bleed
And bigger and bigger grew her evil greed
"*Servant #1 buy me the biggest chocolate cake in the world or you'll get it!*"

"Servant #2 buy me a truckload of caviar or I'll throw a fit!!!"
Gertrude's fits were something her "servants" feared
Her mum, if she had to choose, would rather grow a bushy beard
Her screams would make you deaf and unable to hear
But her parents couldn't simply go "We're outta here!"
For Gertie would hunt them down and scream so high,
That all sense of hearing they had left would go "poof!" and die.
Gertrude indeed was the boss
What should they do, the parents were at a loss
But Gertrude had a secret weakness
Do you want to have a guess?
BOOKS! The girl *(if she could be called one)* hated them so
Just to look at one would make her faint
"Woohoo! It's party time"
The parents would go.
So mum and dad hatched a plot
They would secretly buy, how many books? A LOT!
They would scatter them all around the home
Books about medieval wart-tickling, Books about where dinosaurs roam.
The pair would put them everywhere!
So when Gertie woke up, true came her worst nightmare!
She let out a scream and fled from the house, never to come again
The parents were delighted, they got some papers and a pen.
They invited all their friends to come to their house for a celebration,
But Dad's nasty grandma had come and she caused a sensation...

- Johan Oosthuizen, 12, Londonderry

:BOOKWORM:

Once there was a man,
His name was Professor McJan
He was the smartest person on the Plane
(Except for an Octopus called Janet)
How had he gotten so clever?
READING BOOKS FOREVER!
He read in the morning,
He read when he was snoring
He ate them for his meals *(How crazy!)*
He never moved from his chair *(How lazy!)*
He hated screens of any kind
He would destroy any devices he would find
That was he only time he rose from his seat
To find and destroy any screen he would meet
Janet the Octopus was very clever
Destroy any screens? NEVER!
She knew that if all devices were destroyed
Hospitals, banks, shops, their functionality would be void
So she set on a perilous mission
To save the world, that was her vision

She arrived at the Professor's house
She found a BIG, BIG mouse.
She held it, and it began to bite through the wall,
The wall, indeed, was very tall
At last she managed to break through
She went to the Professor's loo
She hid herself in the narrow pipe
So when the Professor sat on the toilet, the time was ripe
She spread out her tentacles and pulled him in
(He got in easily because eating books makes you very thin)
He was never seen or heard from again
(How easily fooled are men)
But sometimes you can find a book in the loo
It will be boring, that will certainly be true...

- Johan Oosthuizen, 12, Londonderry

:MY JURASSIC WORLD, I LOVE DINOSAURS:

Dinosaurs look like their teeth are big or small or medium,
Dinosaurs sound like the little ones go "roar" and the big ones go
"ROARR",
Dinosaurs feel soft,
Dinosaurs taste like blood and bones,
Dinosaurs smell like donkeys!

- Darwin Overton, 4, Ipswich

:SUMMER:

In summer the wind blows,
In summer the sunflowers bloom,
In summer I happily play,
In summer me and my family paddle at the beach,
In summer is my birthday,
In summer we get hot,
In summer I am adventurous,
In summer I find treasures,
In summer I feel great.

- Seren Overton, 6, Ipswich

:STORM:

Lightning GO!
Thunder ROAR!
Rain POUR!
Wind BLOW!

:SPRING:

The leaves come back on the trees
It was winter, now it's spring
All the colours are coming back
And the sun is shining
And the rainbows come out
The fairies fly around
My heart is filled with joy

- Nivedita Pattni, 9, Kings Langley

:REMEMBERING MY BUNNIES:

Misty light moon bunny
Adventure seeking Poppy bunny
Bunnies hop
Bunnies binky
Bunnies love
Everybody

- Niyati Pattni, 7, Hertfordshire

:ICE-CREAM:

Melty, melty, yummy, yummy
Scrummy ice-cream in my tummy
Chocolate, lemon, vanilla, and peach
Licking an ice-cream down at the beach

- Aibhlinn May Pearson, 8, London

:ALL ABOUT ME:

I am five
Sausages are my favourite food
I like going to the beach
And I love going in the sea

- Ciara Jane Pearson, 5, London

:SWALLOW:

Swooping around the tree tops, a stunt plane showing off.

Whistling on the wires, a calling song.

Acrobats of the sky.

Lightning fast they

Look for a place to make their nest

Or move in to one they made last year

Waiting for the coast to be clear before swooping in to check their
babies.

- JJ Petch, 8, Buxton

:LIMERICKS:

There once was a woman who spied;
Before he had somewhere to hide,
A man with a rake
Who was eating some cake
He saw her and rushed back inside.

There once was a young man who saw
Some pigeons fly in at his door
When he gave a shout
They simply flew out
And left several poos on the floor.

- Beatrix Pilmer, 12, Hampton

:THE POEM OF THE BEES:

Birthday Girl, this is the trees.
Nothing is better than the breeze.
Then all the bees, the bees, the bees
Jumped out of their hive and began to sing
'Flower, flower, this is our hour of sun and warmth'.

- Cordelia Pilmer, 5, Hampton

:THE BEACH:

When I go to the beach
I dive into the sea
It makes me shiver
And my teeth chatter
But I am fine
When I see the sea shine
And the sun comes out from behind the clouds

- Phoebe Piloni, 9, Bournemouth

:FREEDOM:

Diving into the ocean
I feel like a dolphin
My legs become a fin

I fly across the water
Twirling and turning and twisting
The bubbles swoop all around
This is my home
The water unlocks my freedom

- Penhaligon Price-Davies, 7, London

:BARN OWL:

Sometimes I live in a barn,
Or out on a farm,
I won't do any harm,
To you,
Because I prefer to eat a
SHREW!

- Ettienne R, 8

:MARGATE:

When I go to Margate I feel very happy
When I go to Margate the waves swish on my feet and I feel very
relaxed
When I go to Margate I love to crab and fish
When I go to Margate chips are my favourite food
When I go to Margate I love the relaxing sound of the waves
When I go to Margate I swim in the sea
And when I go to Margate I feel just like me.

- Yasmin Reeves, 9

:THE HEART:

The heart in my belly deep down in my belly is full of kindness.

:RAINBOW BRIDGE:

Rainbow is like a bridge.
Rainbow is like a hat.
Rainbow is like a hill.
Rainbow is like a happy smile.

:CLOUDS:

Cloud is like candy.
Cloud is like cloud.
Cloud is like Emma.
Cloud is like good.
Cloud is like a sweet.
Cloud is like candy floss.

- Emma "My Little Pony", 9, Peak District

:BLUEBELL:

Bluebell as blue in a blue, blue forest.
Bluebell forest deep as blue sea.
Blue sea blue, blue as blueberries.

:AUTUMN:

Autumn, Autumn, Autumn.
It's on its way.
Even though Autumn is already here.
But winter,
But winter,
Is on its way.
Even though snow's not coming

- Emma "My Little Pony", 9, Peak District

:SEA:

Seagulls above the sea.
Blue sky against the sun.
Blue as Blue can be.
Blue like the sky.

:THE WINDOW:

I Don't want to carry on not having a view of the seaside.
I will ask my mum," can I buy a window ".
The end.

:THE UNDERSEA:

Blue as blue undersea,
Blue as blue fish,
Blue as blue water,
Blue as a blue carrot,
Blue as a blue bowl.

- Sophie" My Little Pony Lover", 6, Peak District

:POETS STAY AT HOME:

I am a poet and I stay at home.
I like my poems and I like my home.
So, I'm not going to leave,
I'm going to stay home.

- Aletheia Xinyue Ruan, 5, London

:SWEET JANUARY FLOWERS:

How is a flower so sweet and beautiful?
So white and fair?
The bush is so lush and green still,
As lovely as a plant can be.

- Persephone Xinxiao Ruan, 7, London

:MUSTARD AND KETCHUP:

Autumn has lots of colours
Up on the trees.
There are yellows and reds.
Up, the sky is cold.
Mustard and ketchup
Now they are Autumn colours.

- Sophie S, 8, Teesside

They're not alone- hunger and famine,
People acting like salmon
Wembley shudders at the generous life
He wants to clap, but famine is rife.

Jamin' is good
Take off your hood
Like a phoenix burning bright
Praying for the light
Take my hand or let me go
Strikin' hunger my only foe
Take my hand or let me go
Strikin' hunger my only foe.

Author note:
Don't stay quiet
Shout it out
Danger is here
Look out fo'your peer.

- William Simmonds, 12, Whitstable

:QUESTIONS AND ANSWERS:

Questions

Where will you go now everyone you love is gone?

Where will you go now everything you like is wrong?

Where will you go now you're in exile?

Where will you go now your home is no more than a pile?

Answers

Everyone I love is waiting to be called home.

Everything I like is right in my beautiful home alone.

Every day I was in exile while I was here.

Every time I pray I see my home strong and near.

Questions

How do you not wish to show anger and bitterness?

How can you stay strong in times of painfulness?

How will you not bow to sin and evilness?

Answers

I ask my forgiving Father for patience to pray.

I ask my loving King for strength, knowing He cares.

I ask my merciful God for self-control, knowing He is fair.

Questions

Through fights you show your strength and courage, how?

Through cursed speech you show peace and gentleness, answer now!

Answers

My strength and courage come from a strong hold that will never cease.

My peace and gentleness come from the Prince of Peace.

Questions

You will never stop trusting Him, no matter what happens?

Answers

I will never strop trusting Him and I will tell others in paper and pen.

- Taffie Smith, 13, Hornsea

:GROWING:

We are tall and strong
Lord, let us do no wrong
May our roots go deep.
Lord, let your love keep.

We now have roots so we begin to grow
May we grow in numbers as well as rows.

Lord, we begin to start Growing.
Let us remember that your love is all knowing.

- Taffie Smith, 13, Hornsea

:ROBLOX FUN:

Roblox is my favourite game,
It really drives my mum insane,
I talk about it all the time,
But I meet my friends online,
We always have lots of fun,
As long as I get all of my work done.

- Joseph Stanton, 9, Staffordshire

:CLEMENTINE AND THE BOY:

This is the story of Clementine,
A story which I hope you'll find divine.
Clementine lived in the countryside;
She lived a life devoid of pride.
She lived in a cottage surrounded by flowers,
And pancakes and muffins are what she devoured.
Every day she would go into the meadow,
Where sweet-smelling lilacs and lilies would grow.
Her house was perfect, so was her life,
Until one day there came an unexpected strife.
A little boy moved in next door,
And everyone did he ignore!
Clementine wondered what was wrong,
Why he never even liked it when she sang a nice song.
But she didn't have to wonder for long
So she managed to stay curious and strong.
What happened that day,
Is Clementine asked the boy if he wanted to play.

The boy looked sad that day,
But Clementine could see
That the boy was getting angry
So she ran away.

Clementine was upset with how the boy had treated her
And she wanted to know what was wrong with that cheater.
Clementine found the boy crying in the meadow,
Why he was crying she just did not know.
"Whats the matter?" she asked him, in the kindest of ways,
For she had never seen a boy cry, not in a million days.
The boy cried out, "I have no friends!"
Then, in a flash, he went quiet again.
"Well, why didn't you say so?!" was her reply,
"I'll be your friend; friends sure are hard to find!"

So they became friends, and what great friends they were!
And the boy was never mean to Clementine again – ever!

- Hanna Thanweer, 8, London

:DOGGIES:

I love doggies
Doggies very cute
Doggies love kiss me
Love to come to your party
Love cuddle me
Doggies get wet
Paw in my hand
I love to go to my party
I love getting my dress
Boca love her coat
And love her jumper
Love doggies

- Elana Tufft, 3, Bournemouth

:I LOVE PENGUINS:

I love penguins 'cause they're so cute
And they like to build nests in a tree's roots
They're usually black and white
And they sometimes get a fright
And when they do they hoot

They think that seals are very mean
And penguins like branches that lean
They look after their chicks
They live in sticks
And when they're not busy they like to preen

It's hard to believe they live in hot and cold
They live for twenty to thirty years old
They can swim really fast
They never come last
I'd love to have a penguin to hold

- Harrison Tufft, 10, Bournemouth

:GERBILS ARE FUN:

Gerbils are cute
They poo a lot
They need a groom
They like to eat and dig
They're not very big
Sometimes they nibble you
Or they try to run away
I love them a lot

- Maya Tufft, 6, Bournemouth

:THE PERFECT DAY:

When flowers bloom
Bees come out to say hello
Butterflies come out to spread their wings
It's shining outside!

The sun shining down..

All sunny and bright
Perfect outside to swim
Dipping my feet in

The perfect day for me
I hope it never ends.

- Evangeline van Vuuren, 8, Norfolk

:THIS IS THE LIFE YOU CAN HAVE...:

This is my life, what will I choose,
Will I win or will I lose...what will I choose?

I could play video games and watch TV,
All day long but I think I'd see,
That my life wouldn't end up as fun as can be,
I want to be me, I want to be free.

Instead I will explore all day,
Visiting countries along the way.
I'll go to Iceland to slide on the snow,
And watch the Northern Lights glow.

I'll spend time with my family at Halloween,
See friends, eat sweets and have spooky dreams.
I'll do fun things like arts and crafts,
Science experiments and lots of maths.

Cuddling animals all day long and singing them a happy song
Will be the next thing I'll do when I visit an animal rescue.
But the thing I'll enjoy the best of all,
Is dancing and soaring and having a ball.

This is me, I'm feeling free,
My goal is to be happy.
This is the life I will have!
What will you choose, what will YOU have?

- Eliza Varley, 8, Sandbach

:MEMORIES OF SUMMER:

Warm days, warm nights,
Never ending ice cream, beautiful sights.
The trees gently rustling,
The birds were singing.
Me and my mum sitting laughing and chatting.

Gentle breeze in my face,
As we watched the swallows dart and play chase.
It was so hot, we felt on fire –
As the birds started soaring higher and higher.

Lazing on the beach,
Dunes dry and bland.
No sign of the once, fertile land.
Golden sand tickling our toes.
Freckles scattered on mummy's nose.

Mummy and me sitting on the sand,
Listening to the beats of a musical band.
The sun was setting, time to depart.
I'll remember this day in my heart.

Ava Waddingham, 8, Catfield

:MYTHOLOGICAL MEETING:

Hades, Fades and Harry sat on a chair -
In the park with ladies.
Fades said 'Hey ladies! What are you doing?'
The ladies jumped and said 'you're scary!'
Fades grinned and said 'you're hairy!'

:CHRISTMAS CHEER!:

It was the night before Christmas
Santa's sleigh bells were ringing!
The snow globes were glistening
And the angels were singing.
The elves were cheering in their little red clothes,
And Santa was cheering 'Ho! Ho! Ho!'

Ava Waddingham, 8, Catfield

:HALLOWEEN NIGHT:

On Halloween night, it's a really scary fright!
With bats, vampires, clowns and thugs
The black bats could be flying quickly in the dark night
Vicious vampires could be roughly sucking people's
blood
Thieving thugs could be dangerously stealing
jewellery
And the corny clowns could be laughing heavily in plain sight.

These monsters act like vicious villains
You might be hearing screaming "EEKS!"
Sometimes you might hear villainous roars
You might want to take a few quick sneak peeks
They always pick this day of the week
These creatures seek for their revenge, for they want
the most scares

The beasts all look around but no child really cares
If you look closer the children all just look and frown
As the creepy, sneaky monsters find their way inside
In all their houses they tippytoe up the stairs
And give the children quite the scare!
So when you hear the door creek, take a little peek
But only if you dare!

- Bobby Wells, 10, London

:CANDY:

Candy, candy is so handy
Candy, candy sometimes manky
Candy, candy can be sandy
Candy, candy makes me happy!

- Bobby Wells, 10, London

:SPRING EQUINOX - A HAIKU:

Alicorn dances
Through the clear sky. Sparkles,
Into Pegasus.

- Evelyn West, 8, Holywood

:DINO ROAR:

Once I saw a T-Rex come stomp, stomp, stomp,
So I cried dinosaur would you stop, stop, stop?
I was going to him to say how do you do,
But the little T-Rex did a little blue poo!

- Finn West, 4, Holywood

:RAIN:

In the rain
There was a plane
It flew to Spain
I saw a Rainbow through the window pane

- Bonnie Wilgrove Hewitt. 6, Walthamstow

:EVERY TIME I SWIM:

Every time I swim,
Every time I swim,
Every time I swim,
I graze my flipper,
And then it gets better,
And then I swim

:BECAUSE OF WINTER:

Because of winter.
Winter.
Snow.
Clouds,
And sun.
And Snowman.
Because of winter,
Because of winter.

- Olly Wilkinson, 3, Heathfield

:GYMNASTICS BARS:

I enjoy playing on them all day long,
Swinging and twisting while singing a song.
They are red, black, blue and yellow,
Colourful like a bowl of jello.
One bar is short and one is tall.
I really hope that I don't fall!

- Boo Williamson, 8, Bangor

:CHRISTMAS POEM:

Can I open the presents please?
Have some fun with my new RC's.
Right on top of the Christmas tree,
I can see a big star.
Sat on the fire place,
Time is ticking till Christmas day.
Magic Santa sleigh is flying high,
Above in the midnight sky.
Like a ninja in the dark
While silently below,
Children sleep without a peep.

- Jackie Williamson, 12, Bangor

:I HAVE THIS LITTLE PUPPY:

I have this little puppy you see,
Her name is B-E-A-T-R-I-C-E.
She has a crooked tail,
And likes to bite the mail.
With cute floppy ears,
A great sense of no fear.
Her nickname is Bea,
Oh she loves drinking tea.
I have this little puppy you see,
Her name is B-E-A-T-R-I-C-E.

- Katelyn Williamson, 13, Bangor

:MEADOW MEANDERS:

Walking for hours
Admiring the flowers
Blue is for Speedwell
And beautiful Bluebell
Goldfinches on Sorrel
Hedges of Laurel
Bindweed coiled
Round Bird's-foot-trefoil
Fields of Red Campion
And Round-headed Rampion
Star-shaped Borage
Ready to forage
Candyfloss Common Bistort
Cinnabars on the Ragwort
Tall yellow Tansy
Tiny purple Pansy
Scarlet Pimpernel growing low to the ground
In certain places there's plenty to be found
Forget-me-nots short and foxgloves long
Growing by the coast is pink Hound's-tongue

- Luna Wilson, 9, Stoke-on-Trent

:MY PETS:

Lucky is my black and white cat
He likes his food and is getting fat
Plooshy is ginger and brown
He is the slinky cat about town

The cats were born on my Daddy's birthday
We brought them home on a sunny day
We gave them food and watched them play
In their new home in which they will stay

Lucky likes to climb the tree
I sometimes watch while I drink my tea
Plooshy likes to curl up in a ball
He sleeps, he dreams, he purrs, that's all!

We think that Lucky fell out of the tree
He thought he could fly, but it wasn't to be
He broke his leg and ended up at the vet
And now there is a metal plate in my pet

Lucky and Plooshy go out for the day
But at night they come home and with us they stay
With my hamsters and fish which live in my room
Which we hope won't be dinner for my cats sometime soon!

- Oscar Woolford, 10

: M Y G I R L :

my girl – phr. the bittersweet feeling of coming home to oneself.

we still have sharpie on our legs from the summer

reading Keats underneath the cherry blossom blush

your signature left a red mark on the skin of my thighs

we weren't thinking straight, but i sketched you out in my head

on many nights, over and over and over and over and over

until i was too far gone, absorbed in our fabrications

my girl is so tantalising, gold rush at my fingertips

my girl is a goddess, golden rays on milky skin

i don't want to leave her, but the city's calling me

nothing is ever real until it is experienced

and i want to experience the calloused corners

i want to show you the backstreets,

tripping over shoe laces, chewing gum at 4pm

my girl is coming home again

- Eva Woolven, 12, Mildenhall

:M Y B L O O D :

my blood is prettier than your blood

it's sacrificial, slim pickings,

cartilage, tendons

cut me open and it's tender

my bones are raw, what about your bones?

my spine, my eyes my skeletons

count me up like an abacus

and string up the remainder

my only attribute

there's cracks in the porcelain

of my pretty bones

and i want to stay at home

and watch the rain dilute my blood

- Eva Woolven, 12, Mildenhall

:AUTUMN IS BEAUTIFUL:

The leaves falling down,
The colours change,
It's so beautiful,
I like the cakes.

I like the fireworks,
Not the sound,
I like fireworks in the garden,
I like leaves on the ground.

- Clara-Elizabeth Worton, 4, Stockton-on-Tees

:I LOVE MINECRAFT:

Bedrock's at the bottom of the world,
Minecraft is fun,
Alex and Steve are in Minecraft,
Yellow's the colour of the sun.

Spawn on just a tiny island,
And you're unlucky,
If you spawn somewhere with mud,
You'll think 'mucky!'

The crazy thing is there's mobs,
Witches have splash potion,
Zombies, skeletons and spiders,
Skeletons have shooting motion.

Sometimes you'll spawn with a chest to start with,
With oak plants you'll be glad,
Baby villagers are cute,
Zombies and witches are bad.

- Finlay Worton, 6, Stockton-on-Tees

:AUTUMN LEAVES:

Autumn is coloured,
With orange, yellow, brown and red,
Autumn is beautiful,
Leaves fall on my head.

- Finlay Worton, 6, Stockton-on-Tees

Back, back, backedy back I've just finished school,
Back, back, backedy back I'm coming through the door,
Back, back, backedy back I'm going up the stairs,
Back, back, backedy back I'm in my room again,
Back, back, backedy back I go to bed and then...
Up, up, uppity up it's morning time again.

- Joshua, 8

A fish playing Minecraft, flapping on the keyboard
Walks in a lava pit
And the world explodes!!!

- Zachary, 6

:IN THIS TOGETHER:

To any child out there who feels like me
That no other children write poetry
We are all here, some hiding, some not
Some praised and rewarded, some sadly forgot
Any type of poems, we write them all
We have our victories, we have our falls
So even though many of us you won't ever see
We're in this together; you, them and me

We are all here, some hiding, some not
Some praised and rewarded, some simply forgot

- Jet, 12

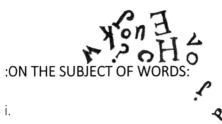

:ON THE SUBJECT OF WORDS:

i.

Words hide behind dams
Recoiling from the very idea of
Ink, spattering them onto paper
Trembling at the very thought of being crossed out
Edging away from fingers, grasping for inspiration
Rolling away from the tongue, causing a
Stutter of short, sullen poetry, with no sense at all

Blocked behind a wall, waiting for the traffic lights to change
Lines of inspiration jostle
Overspilling into the wastepaper basket
Chains of thoughts and ideas leaping fruitlessly up and down
Knowing it is hopeless to try and jump onto the top of the writer's
        block

ii.

The word trembles, knowing its fate
It's inked onto paper riddled with holes,
Now - the same pen that wrote its existence to date
Is poised to scrape through its long-faded lettering

Its pronunciation will grow strange to the tongue
Its script unsure to the eye
As the judgement bearing nib descends
The word gulps
"I don't want to die!"

- Jet, 12

Printed in Great Britain
by Amazon

14995125R00120